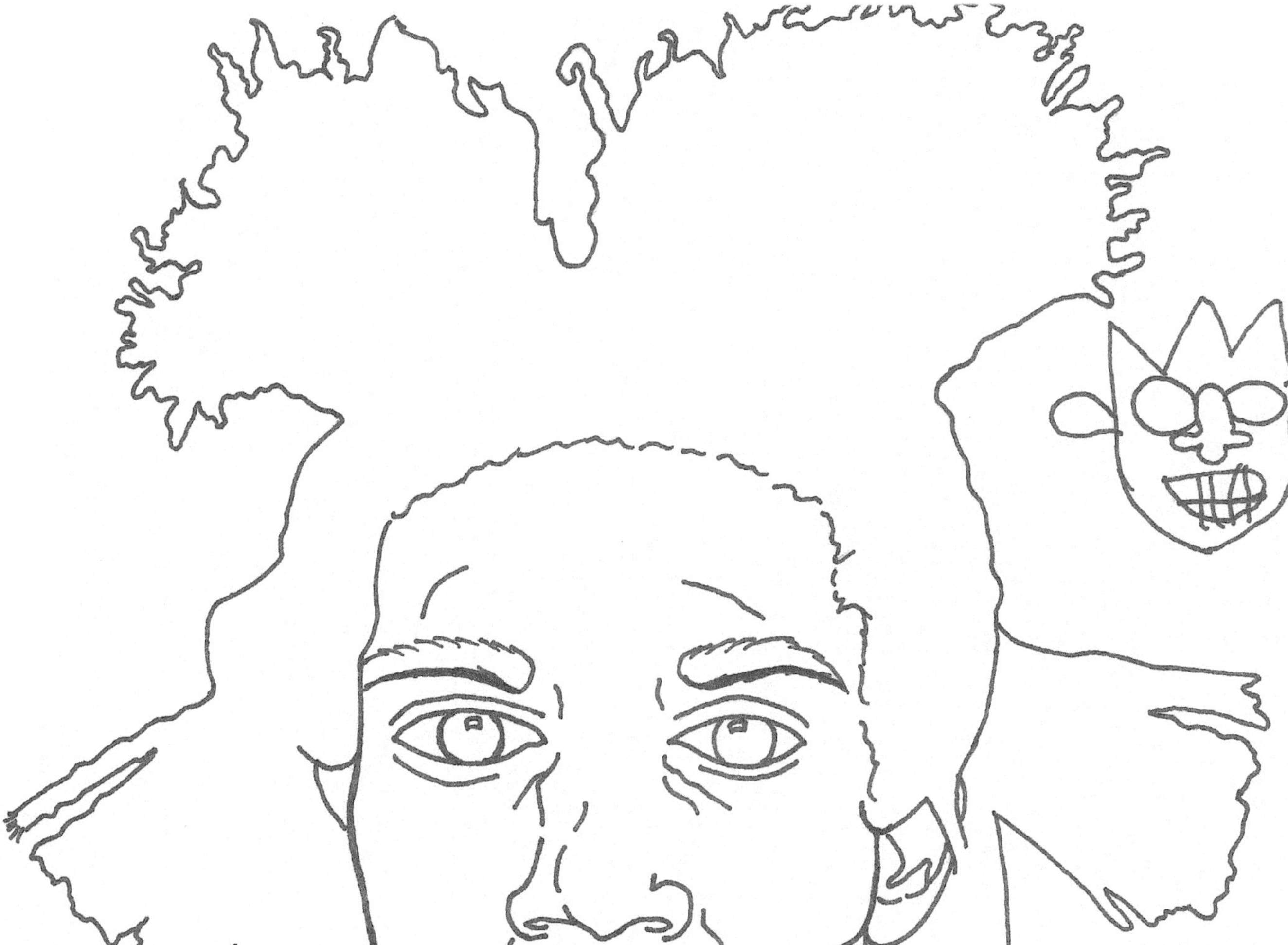
JEAN-MICHEL
BASQUIAT

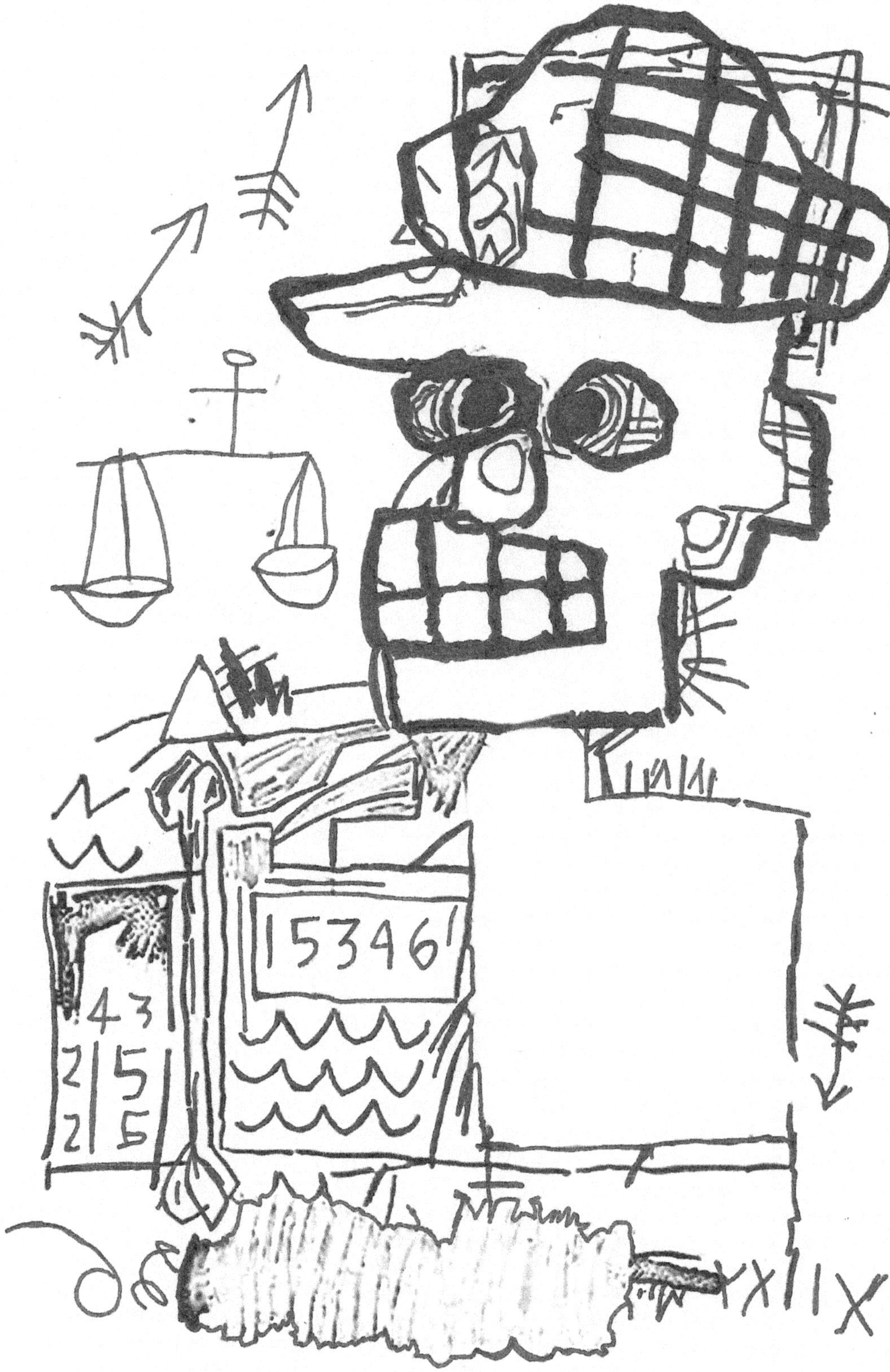
15346'
43
2 5
2 5
XXIIX'

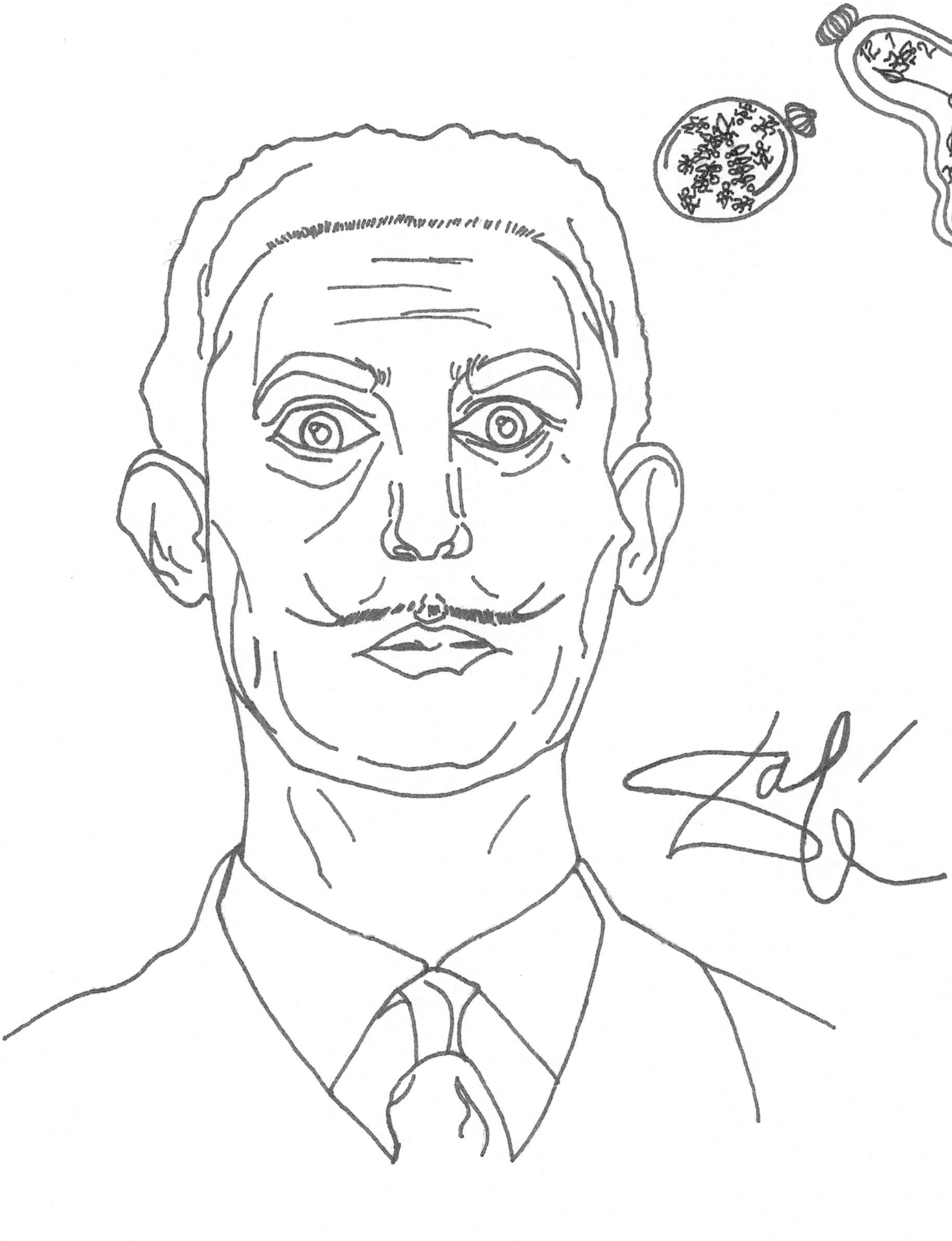
Dalí

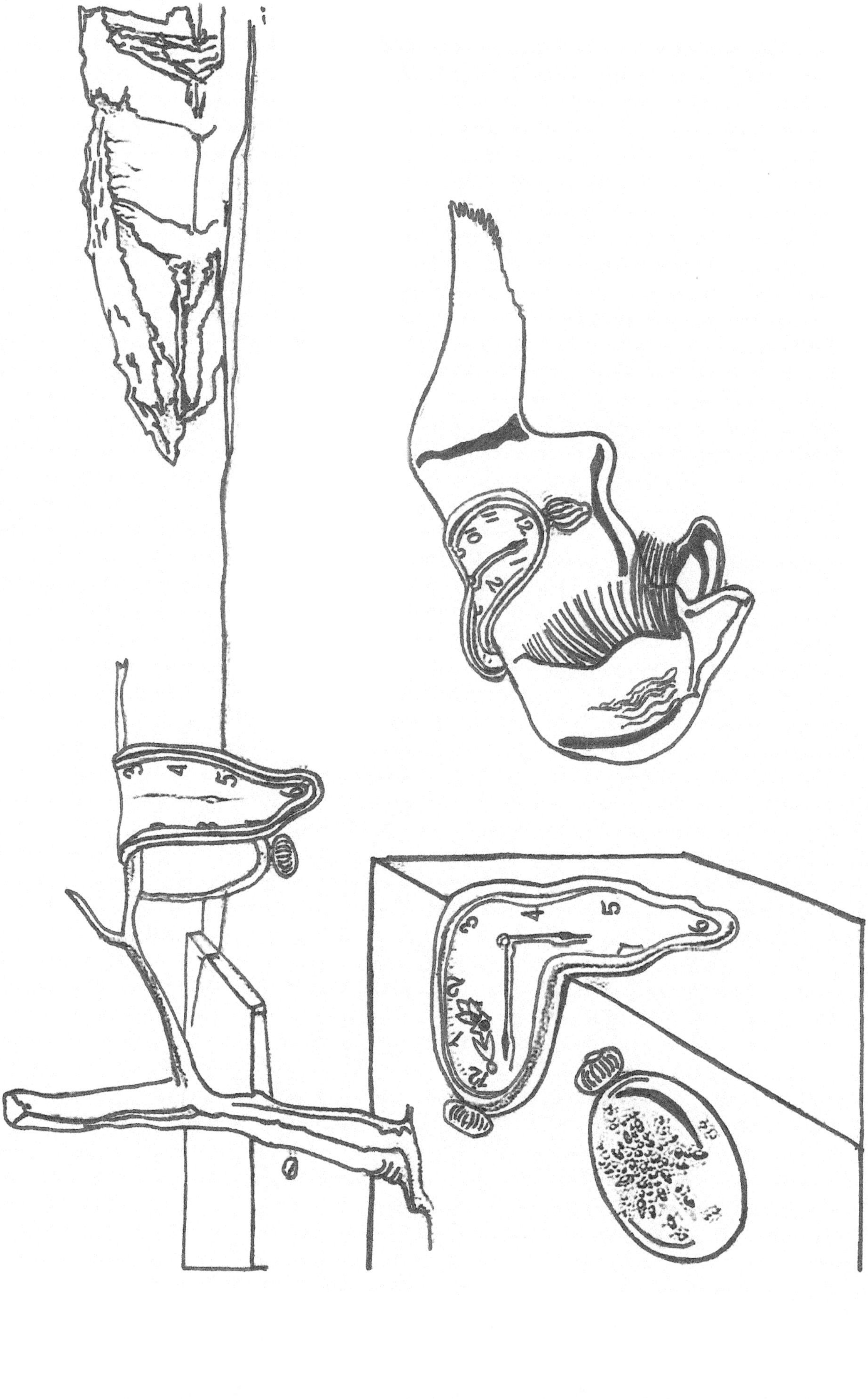

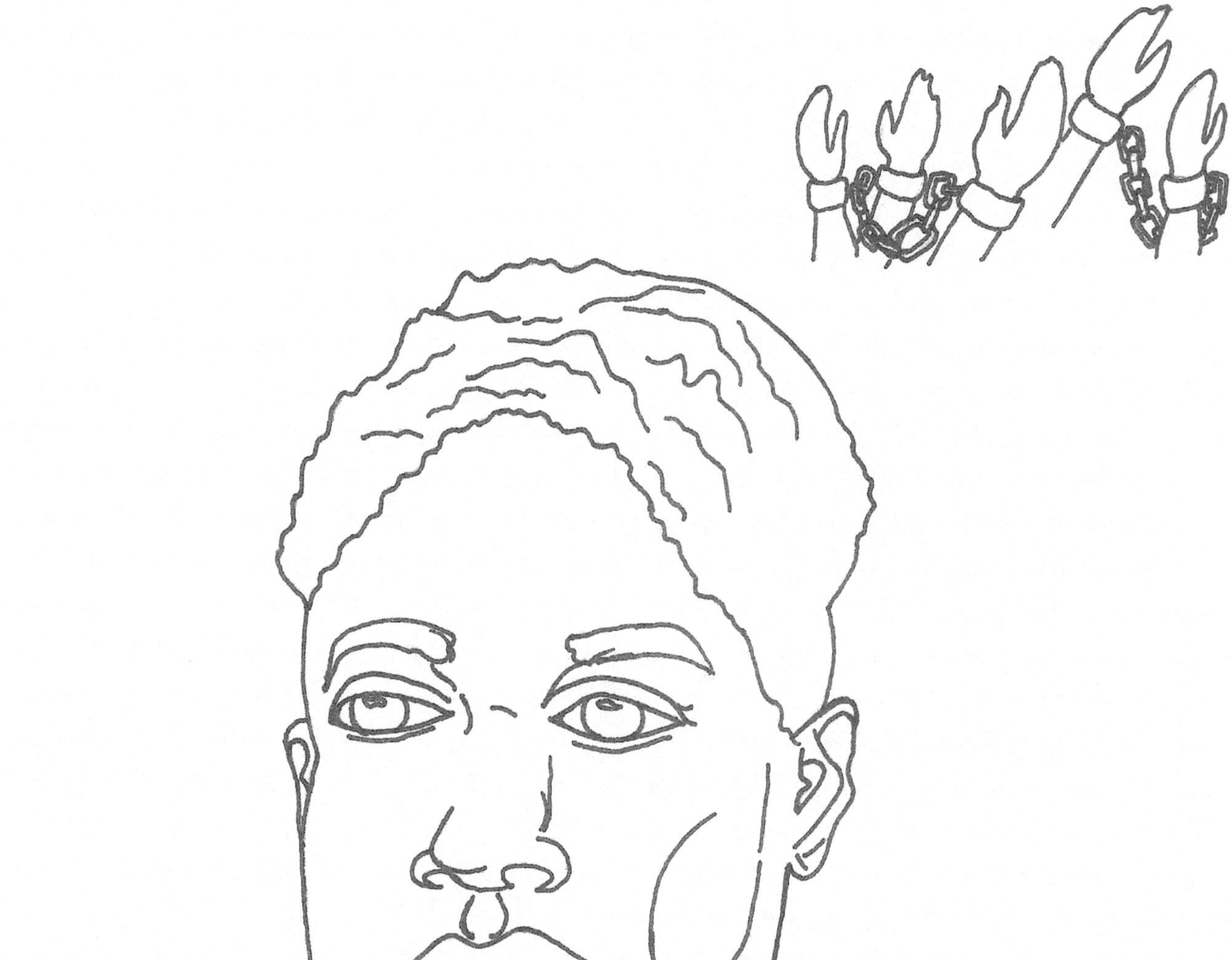
A. Douglas

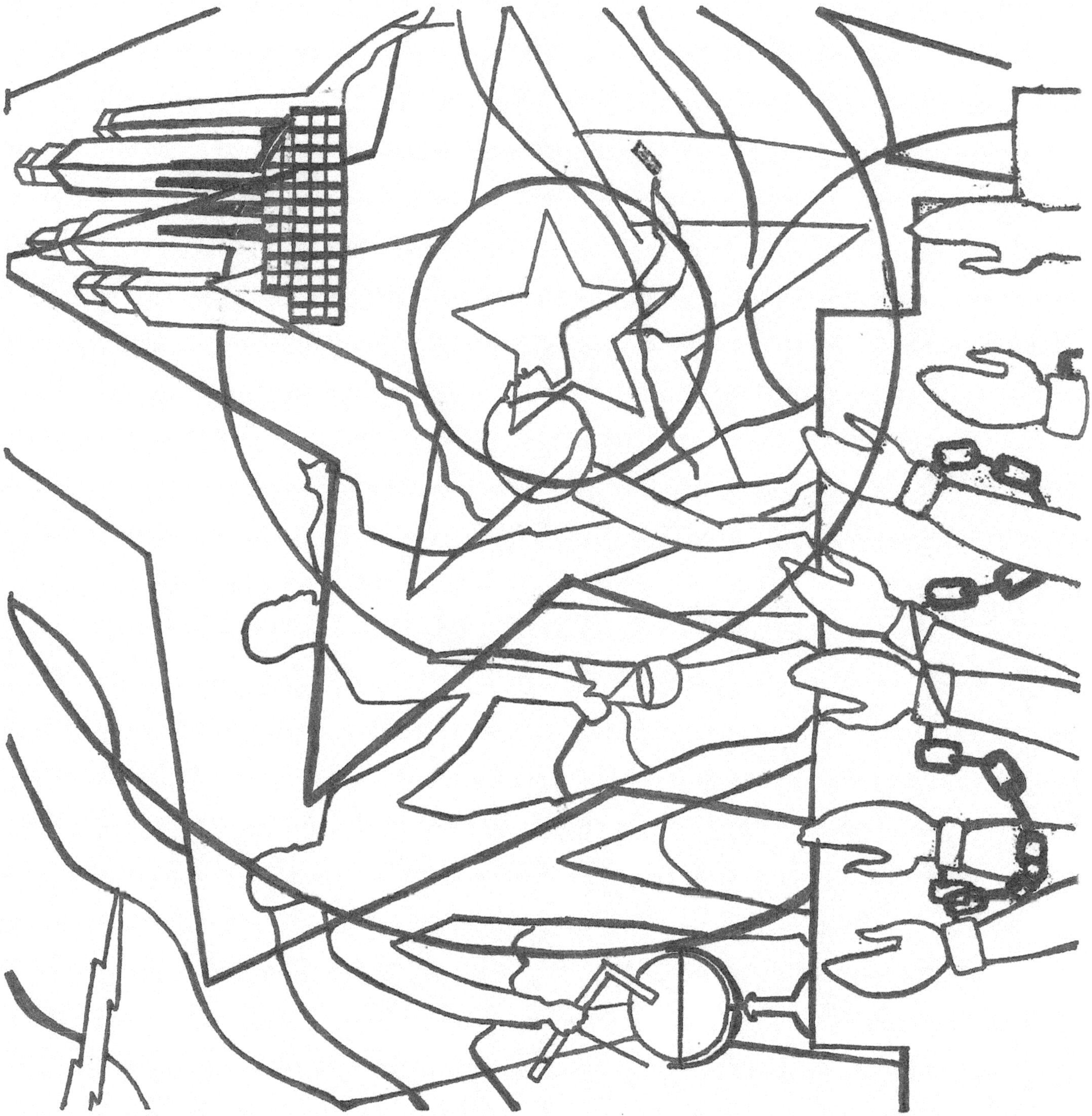

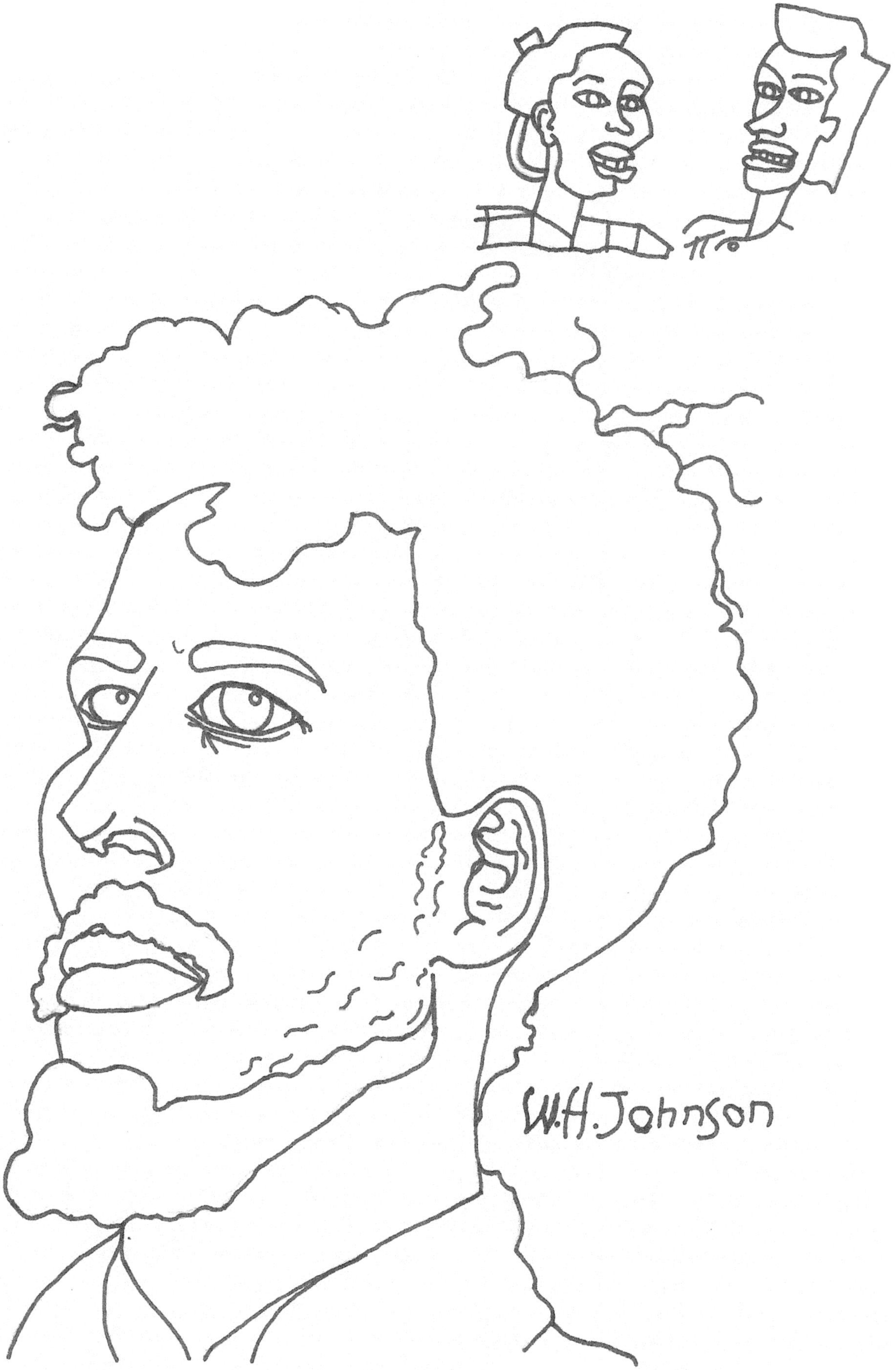
W.H. Johnson

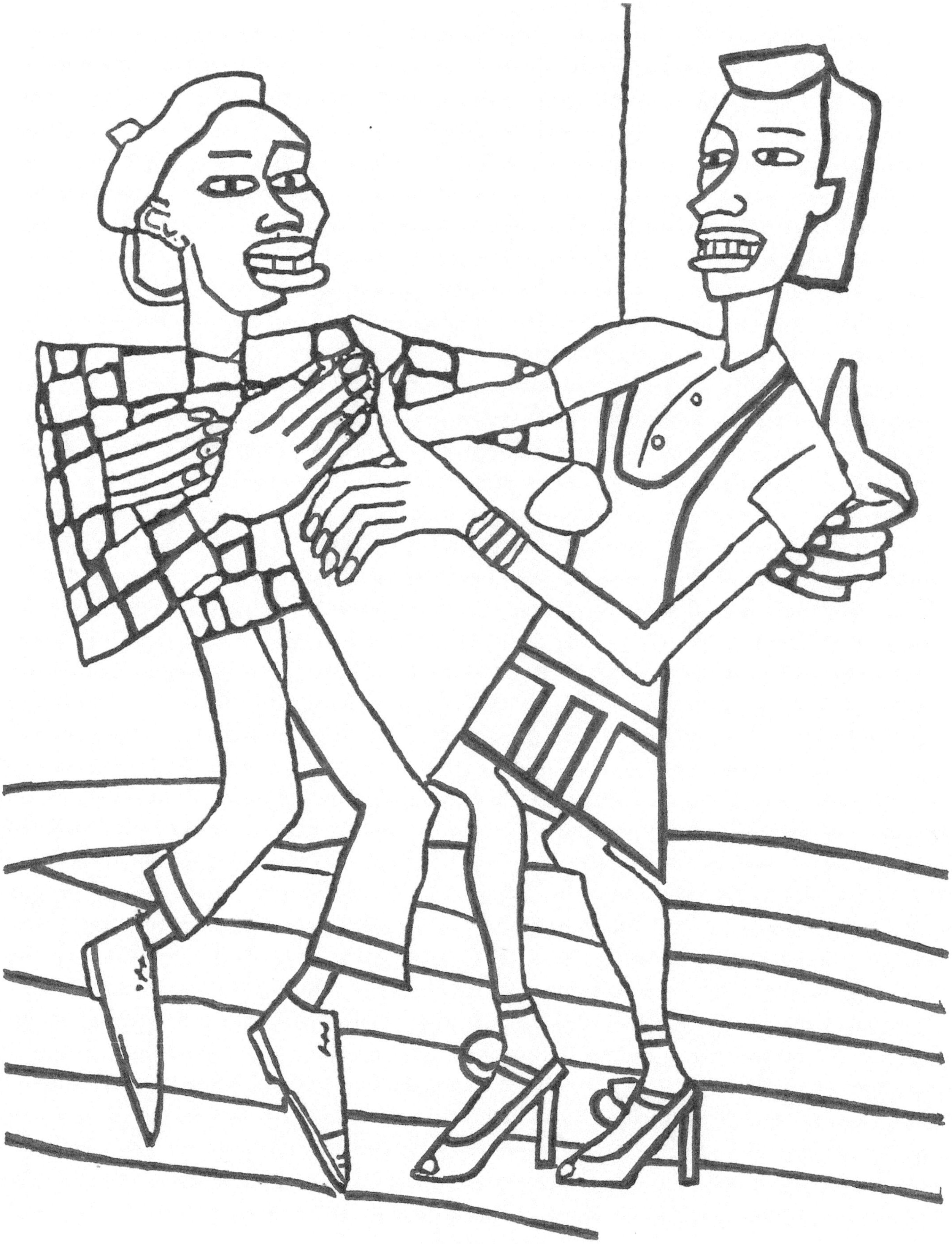

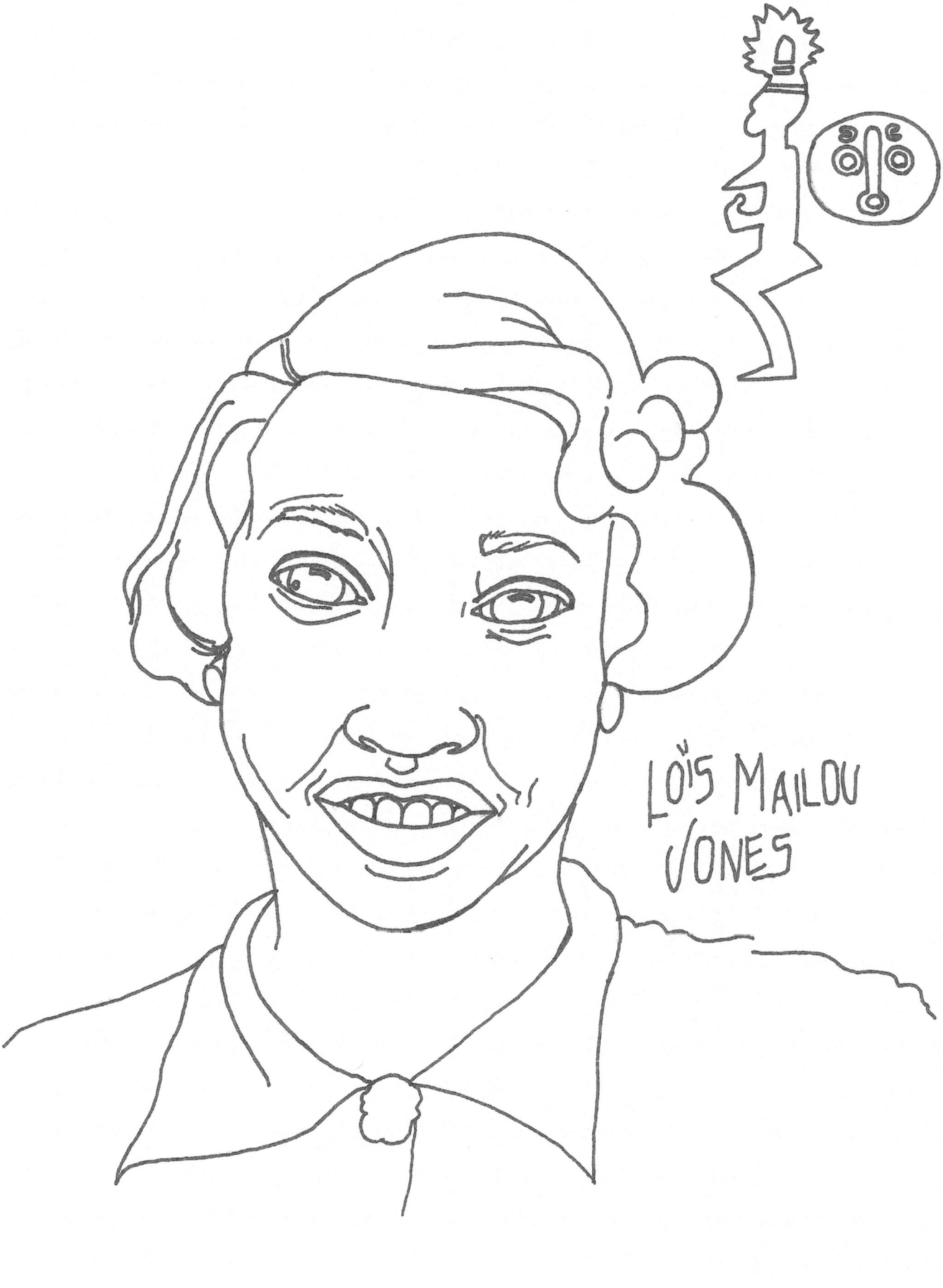
LOÏS MAILOU
JONES

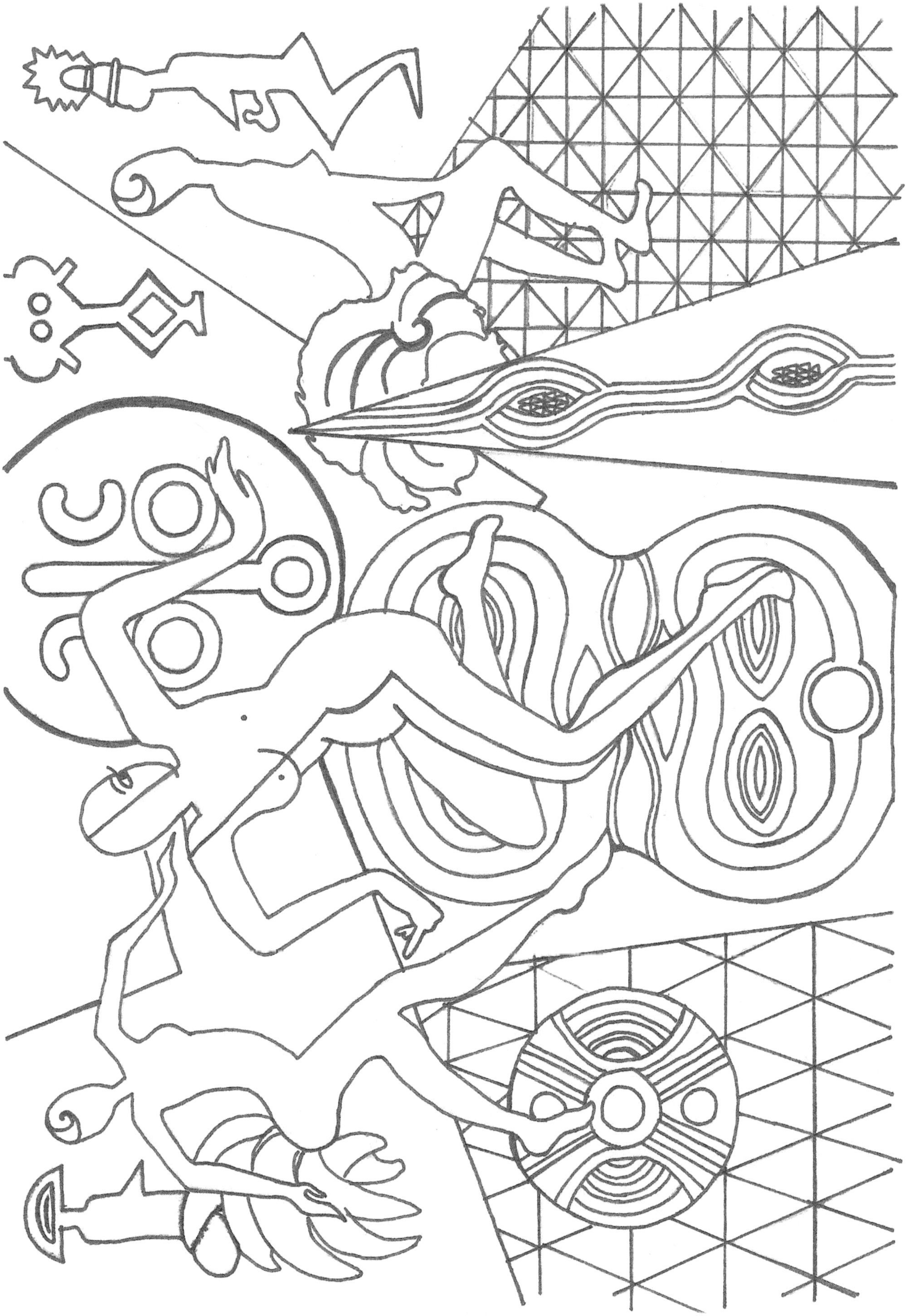

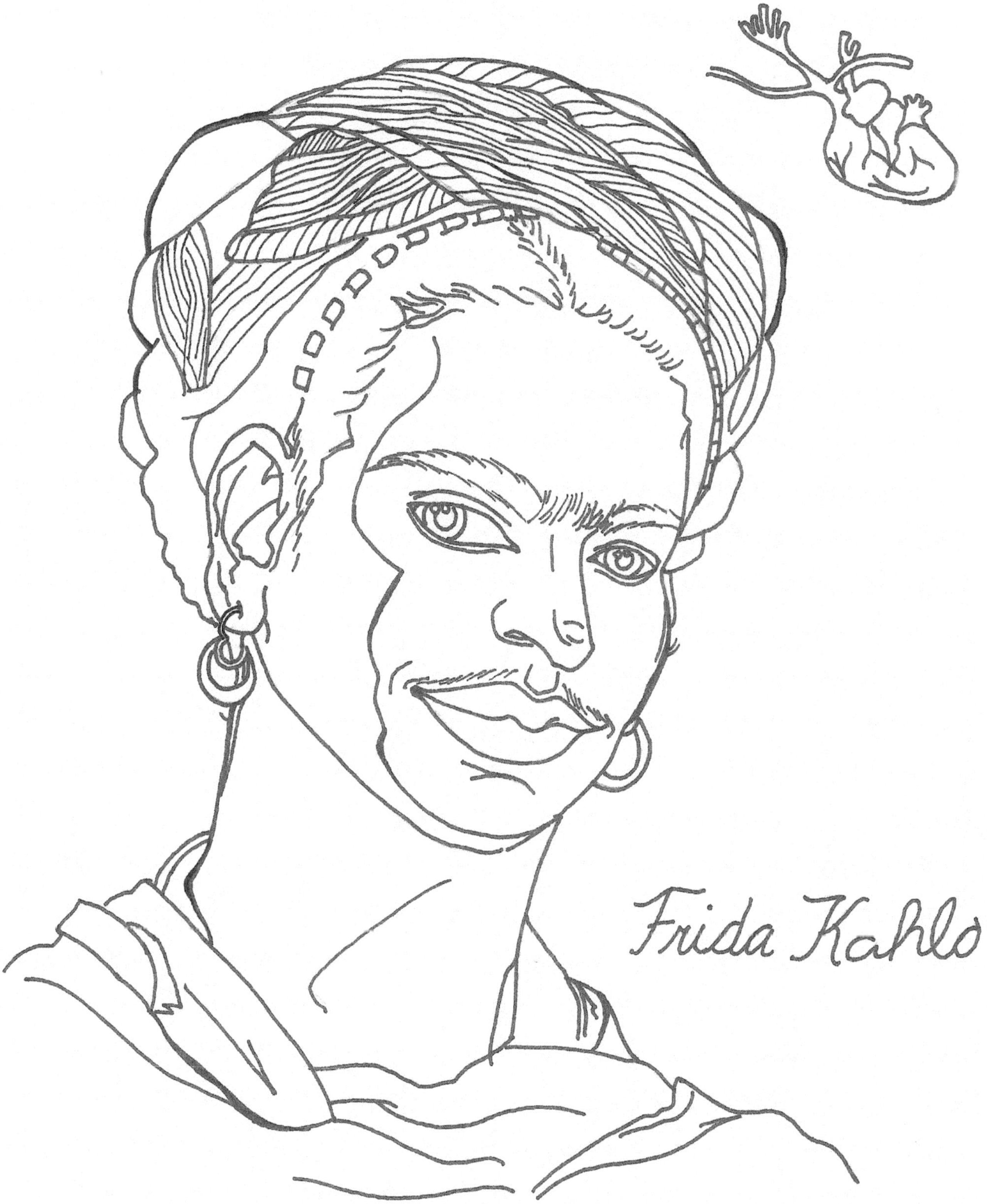
Frida Kahlo

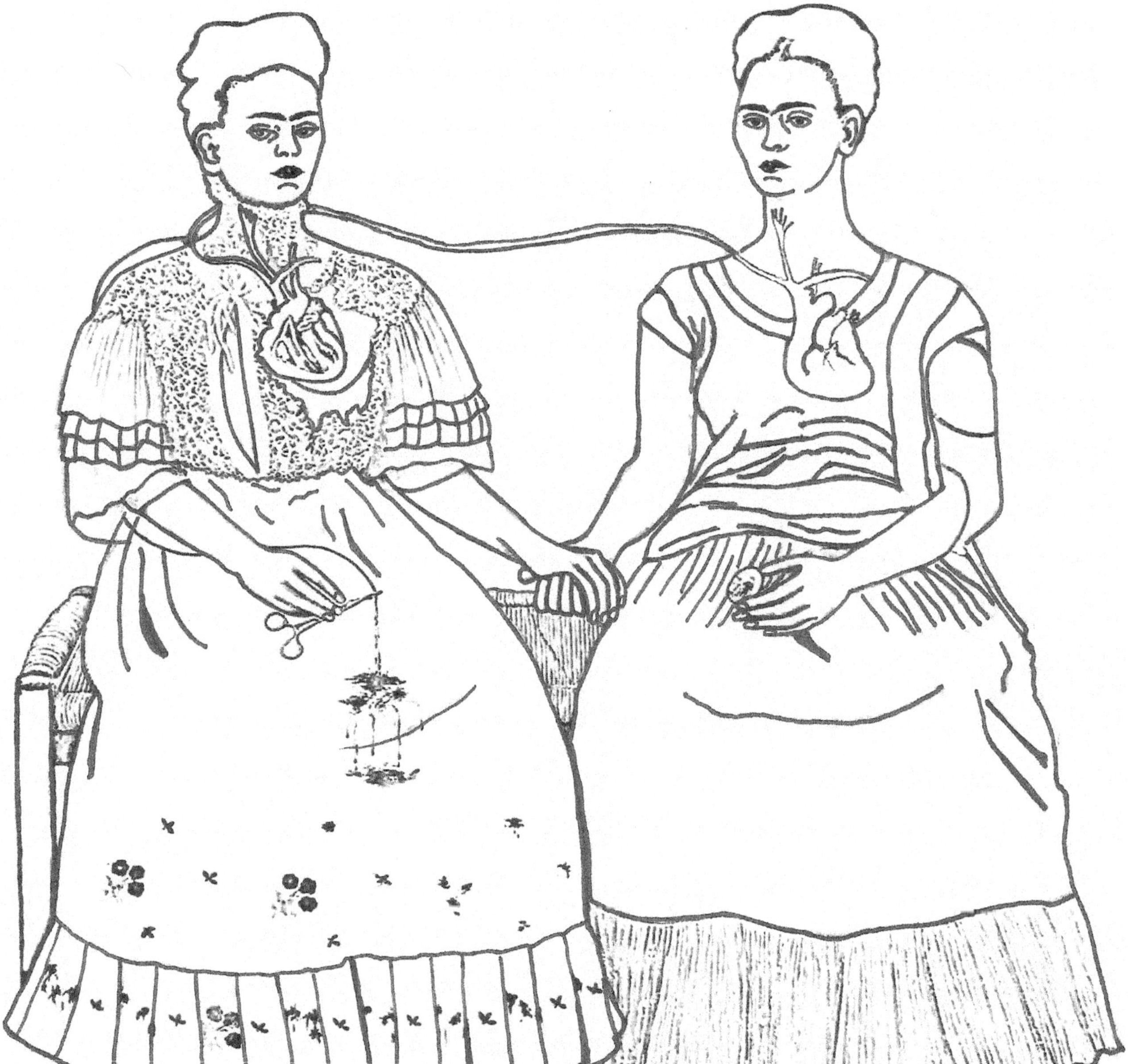

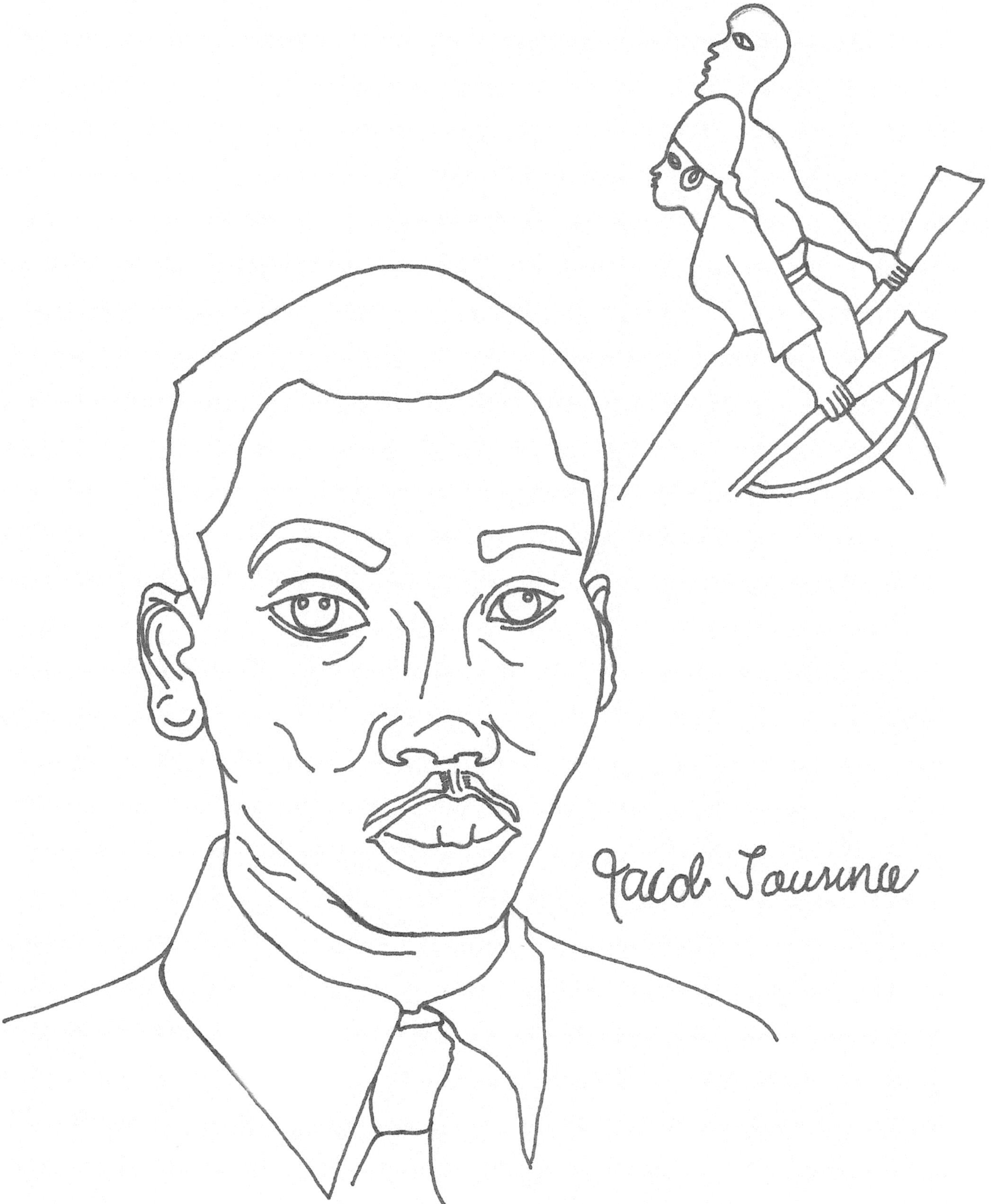
Jacob Lawrence

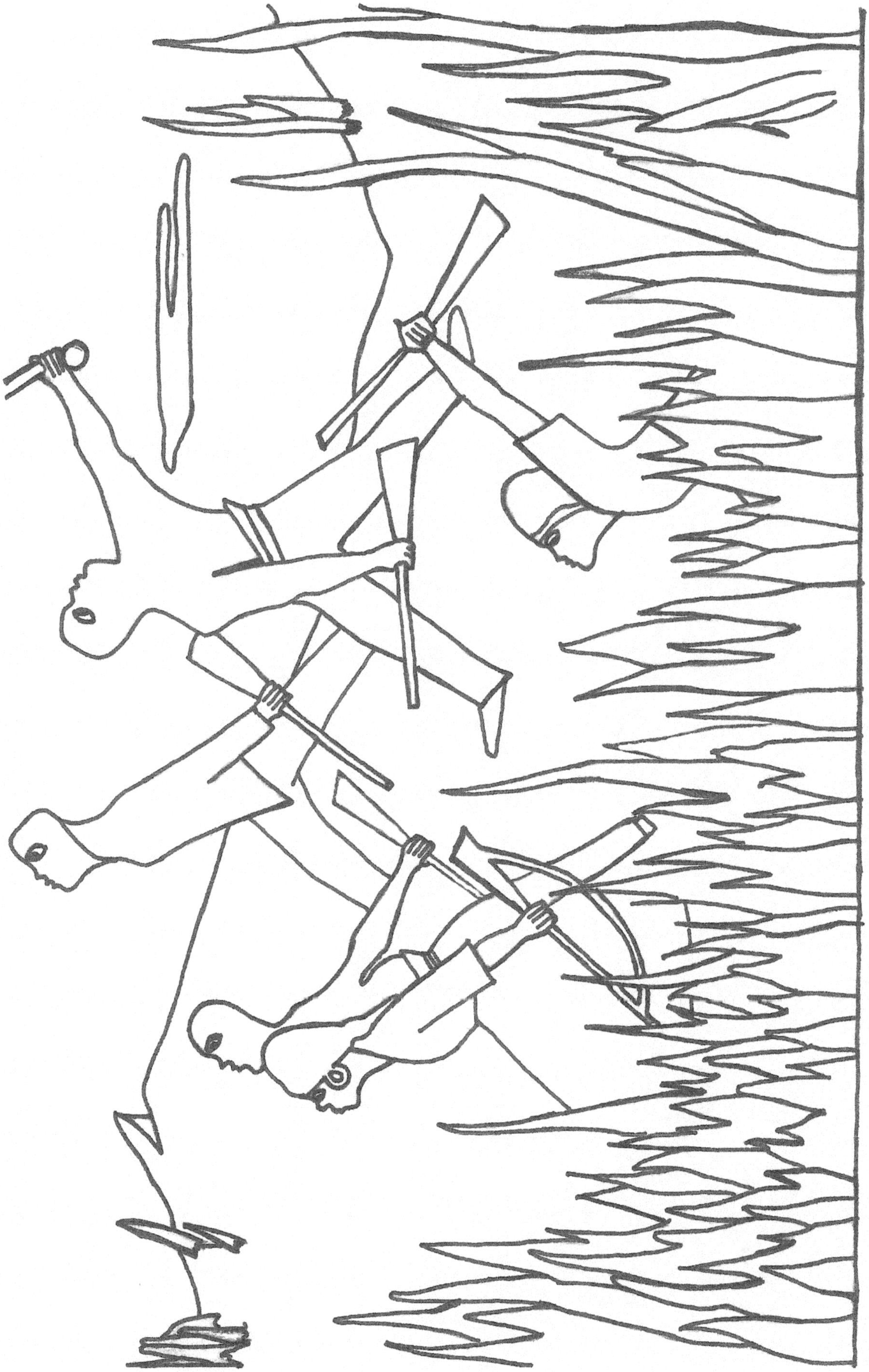

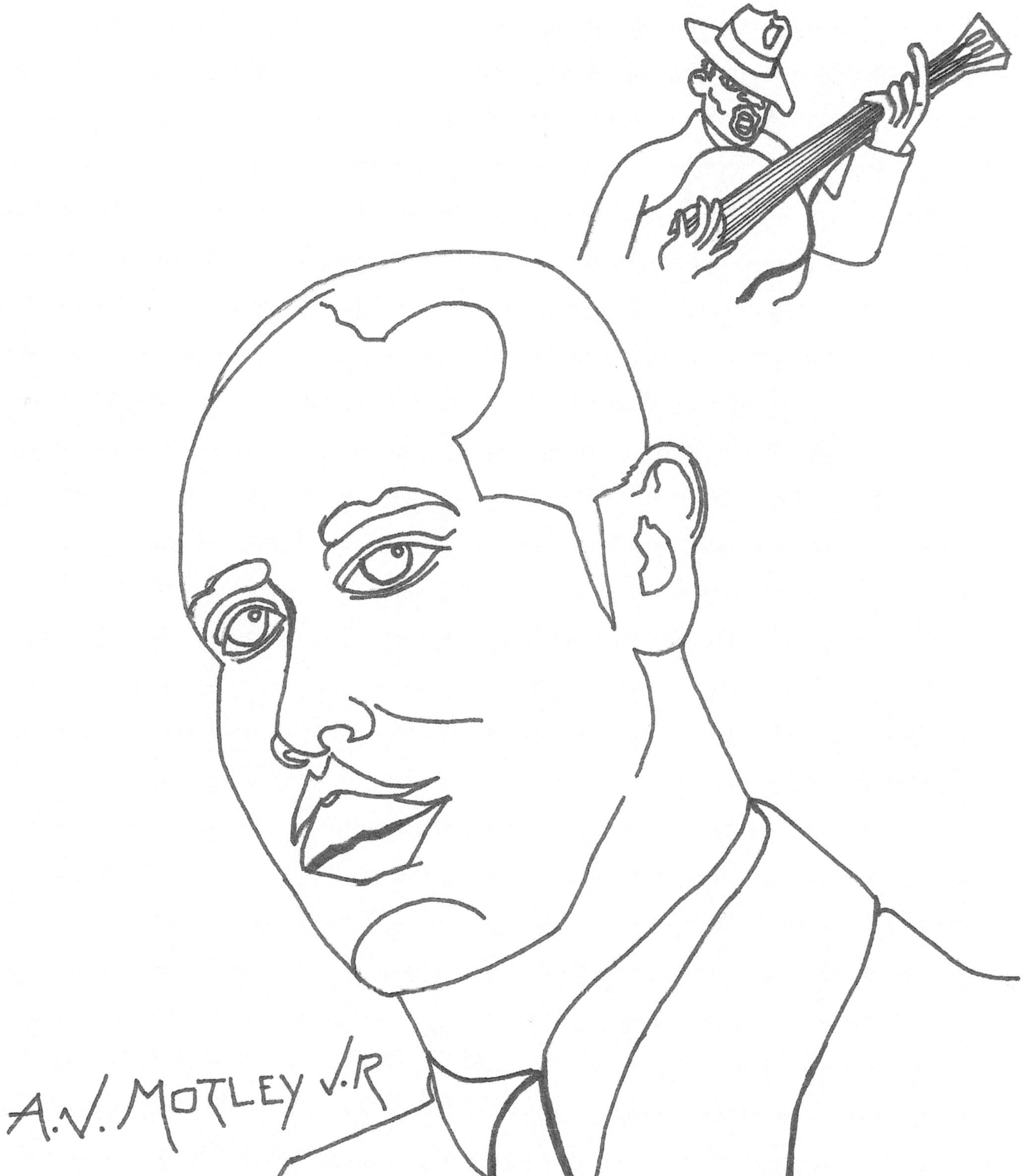
A.V. MOTLEY J.R

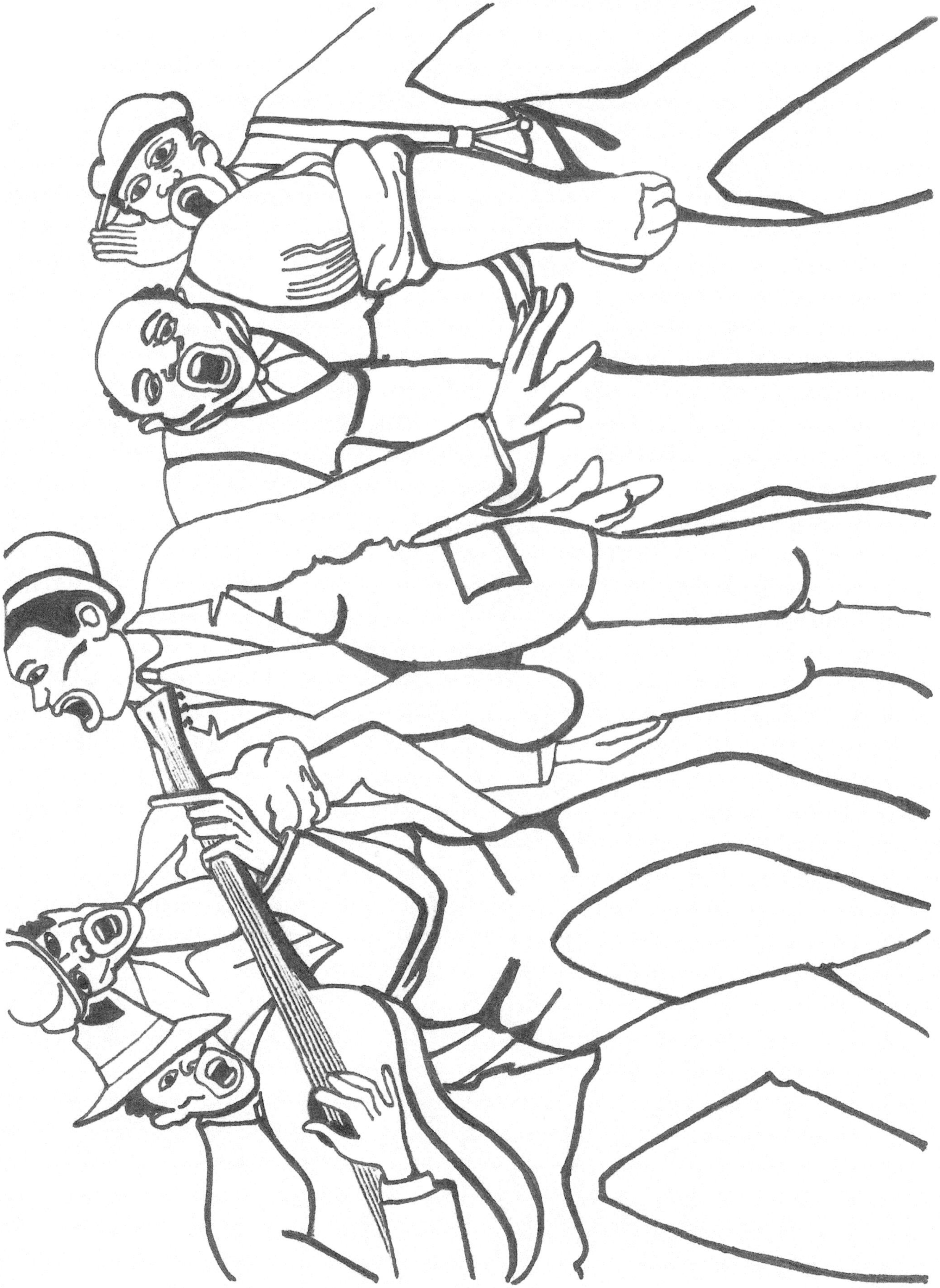

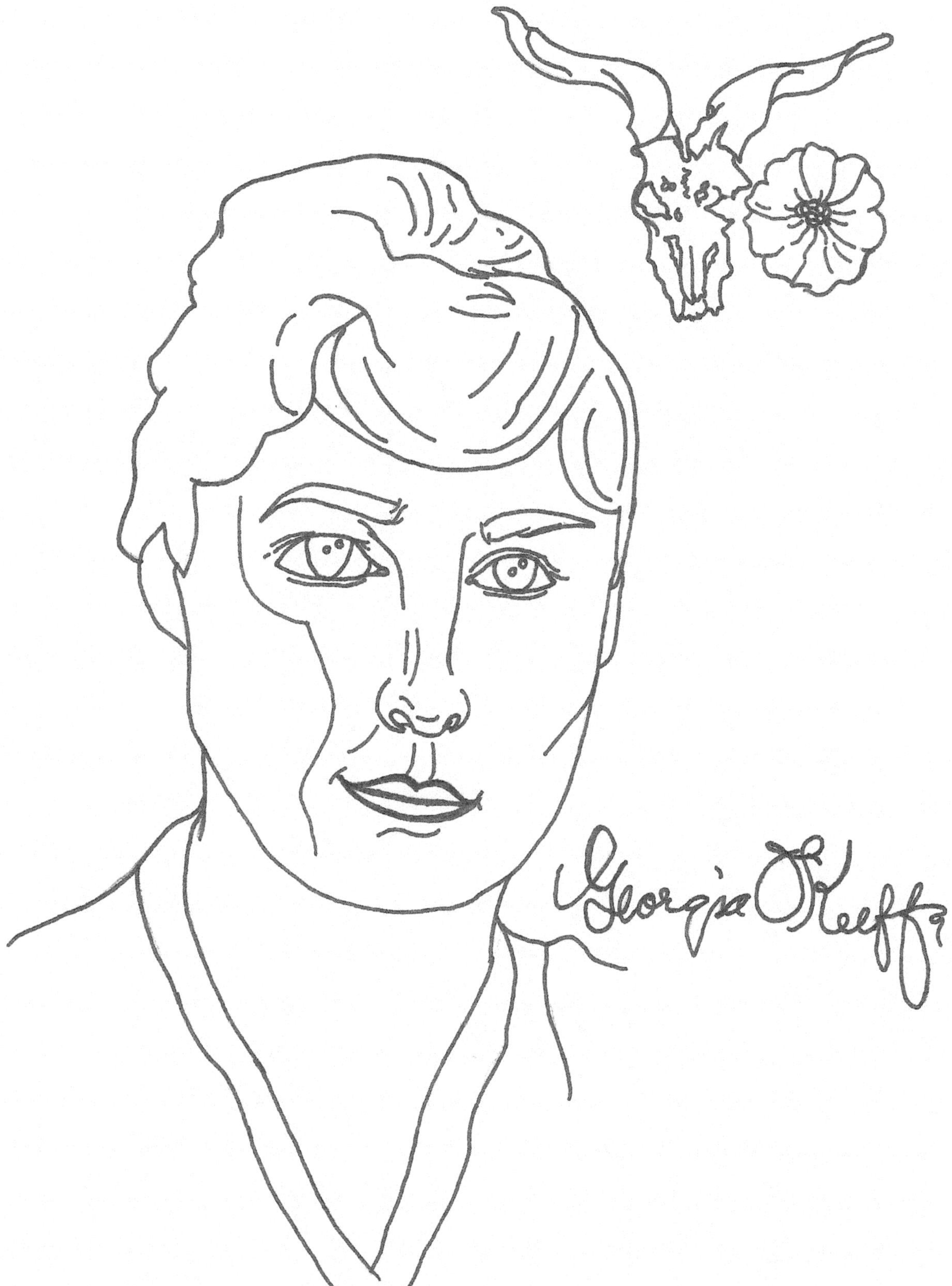
Georgia O'Keeffe

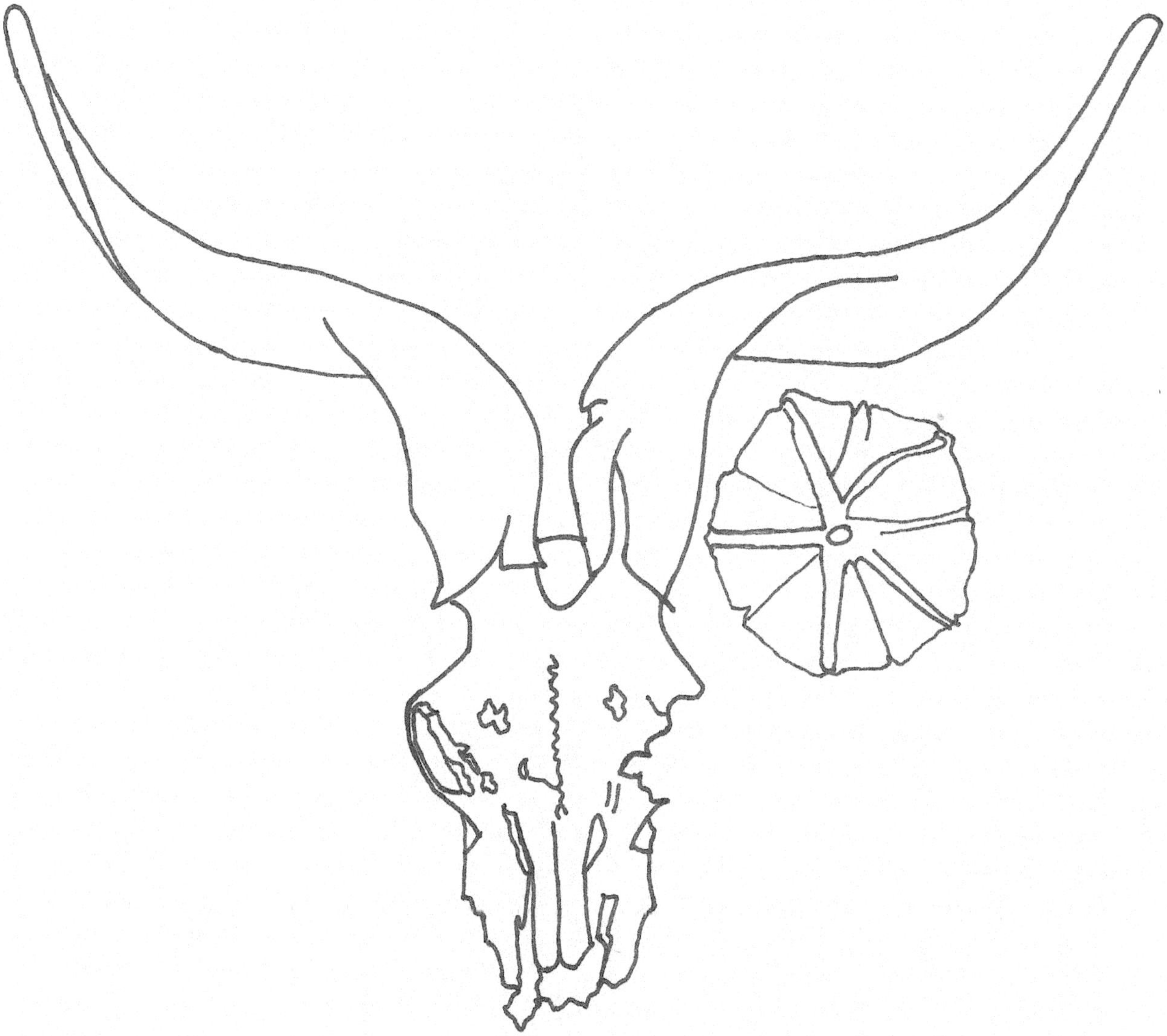

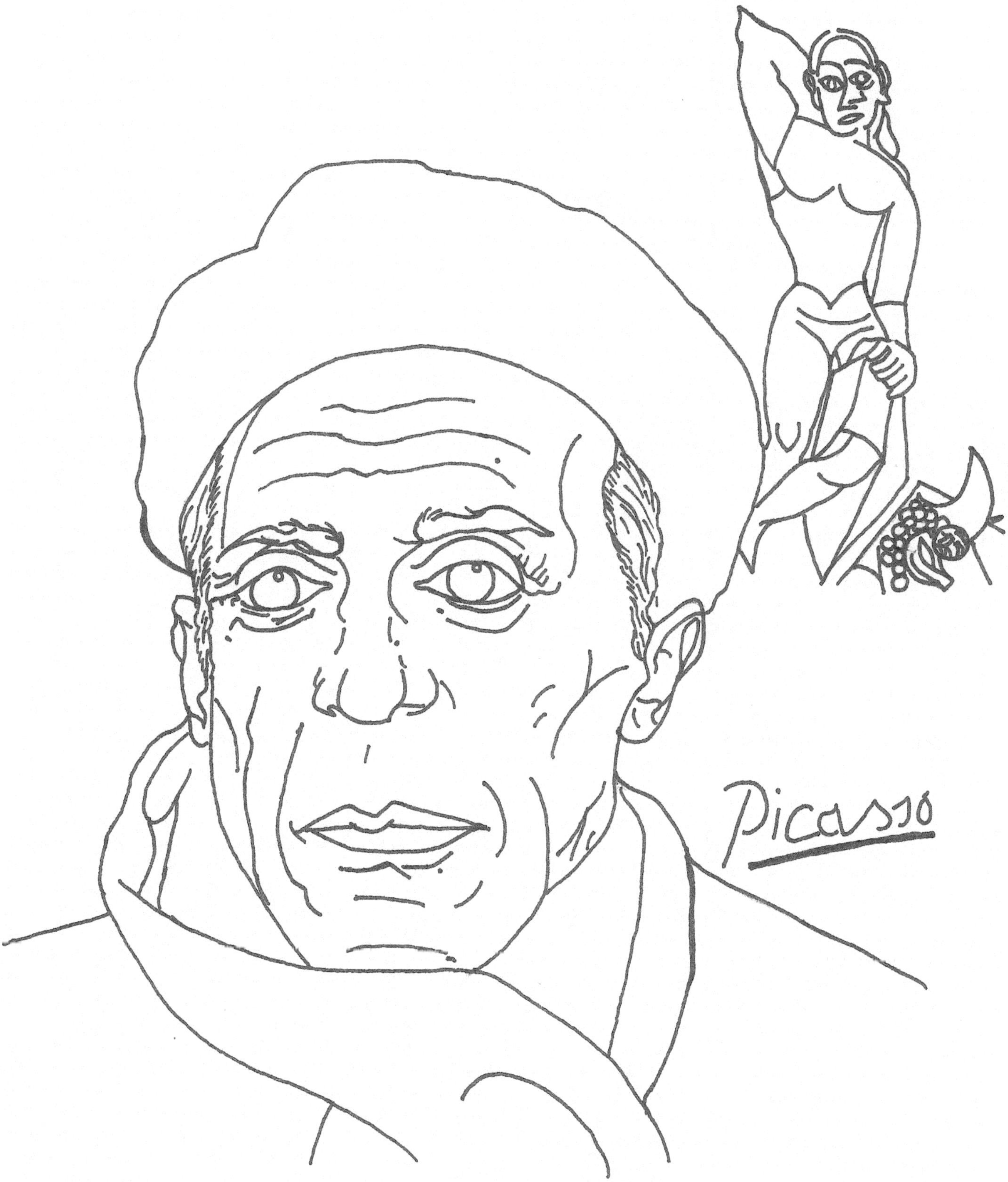
Picasso

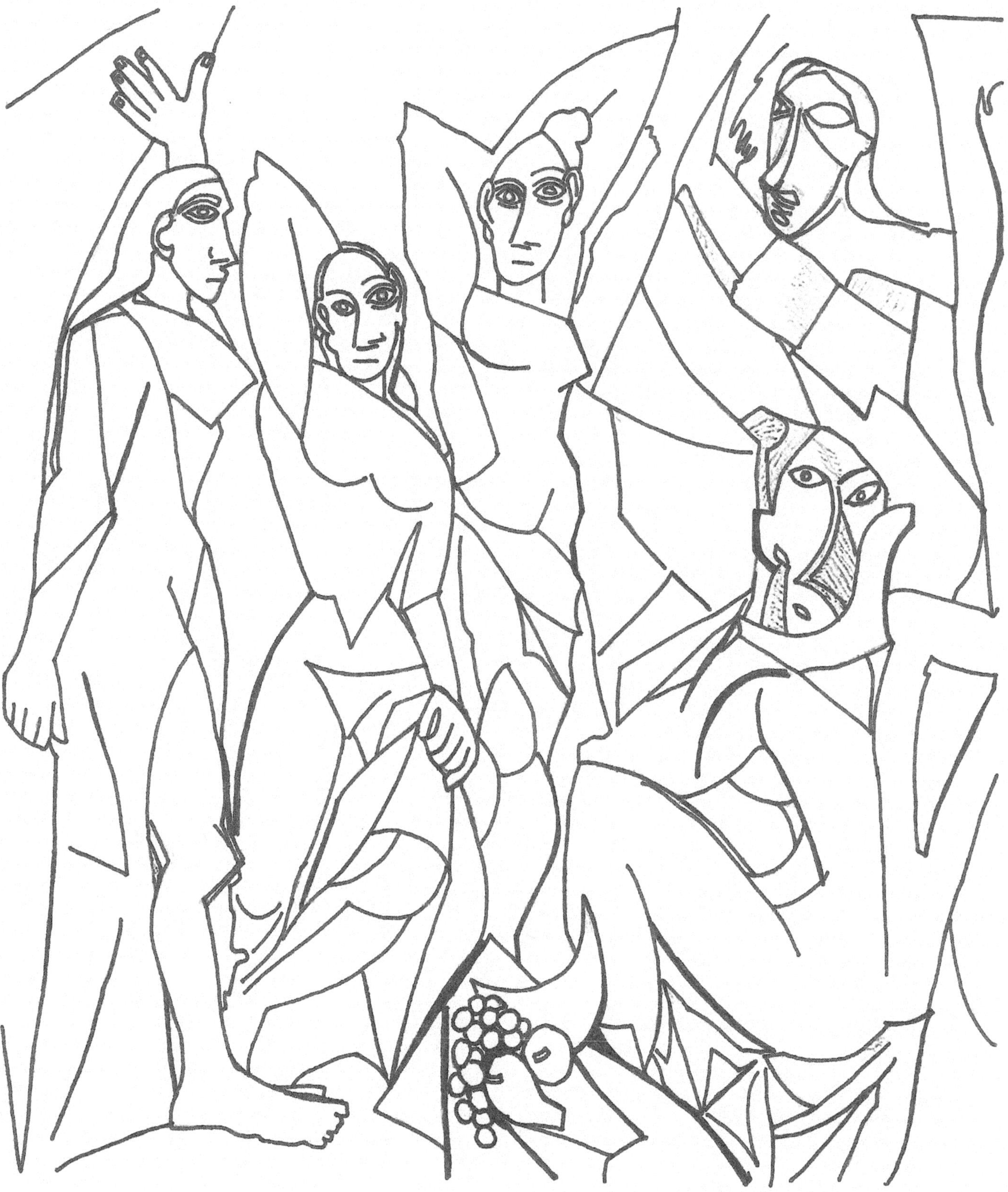

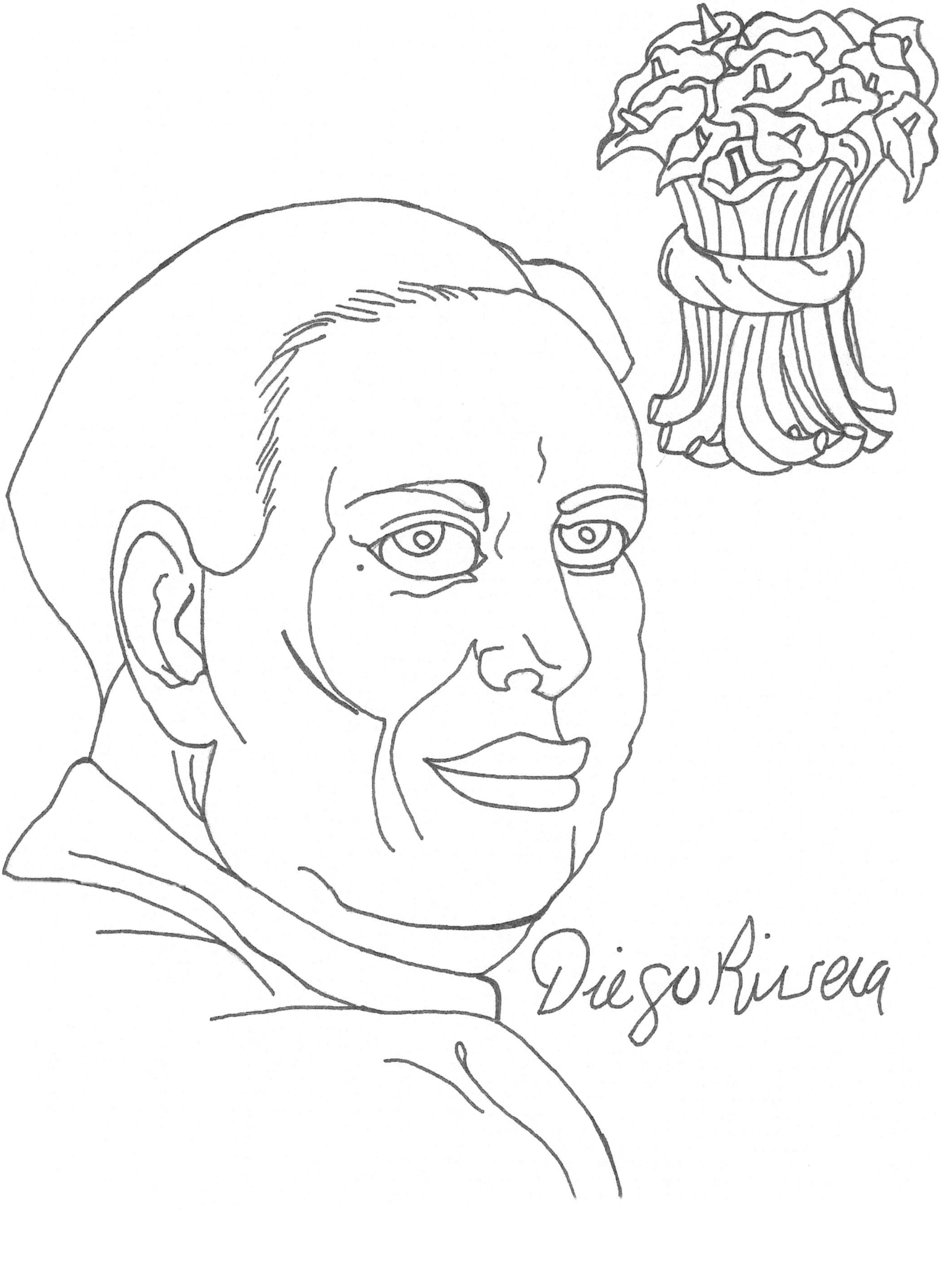
Diego Rivera

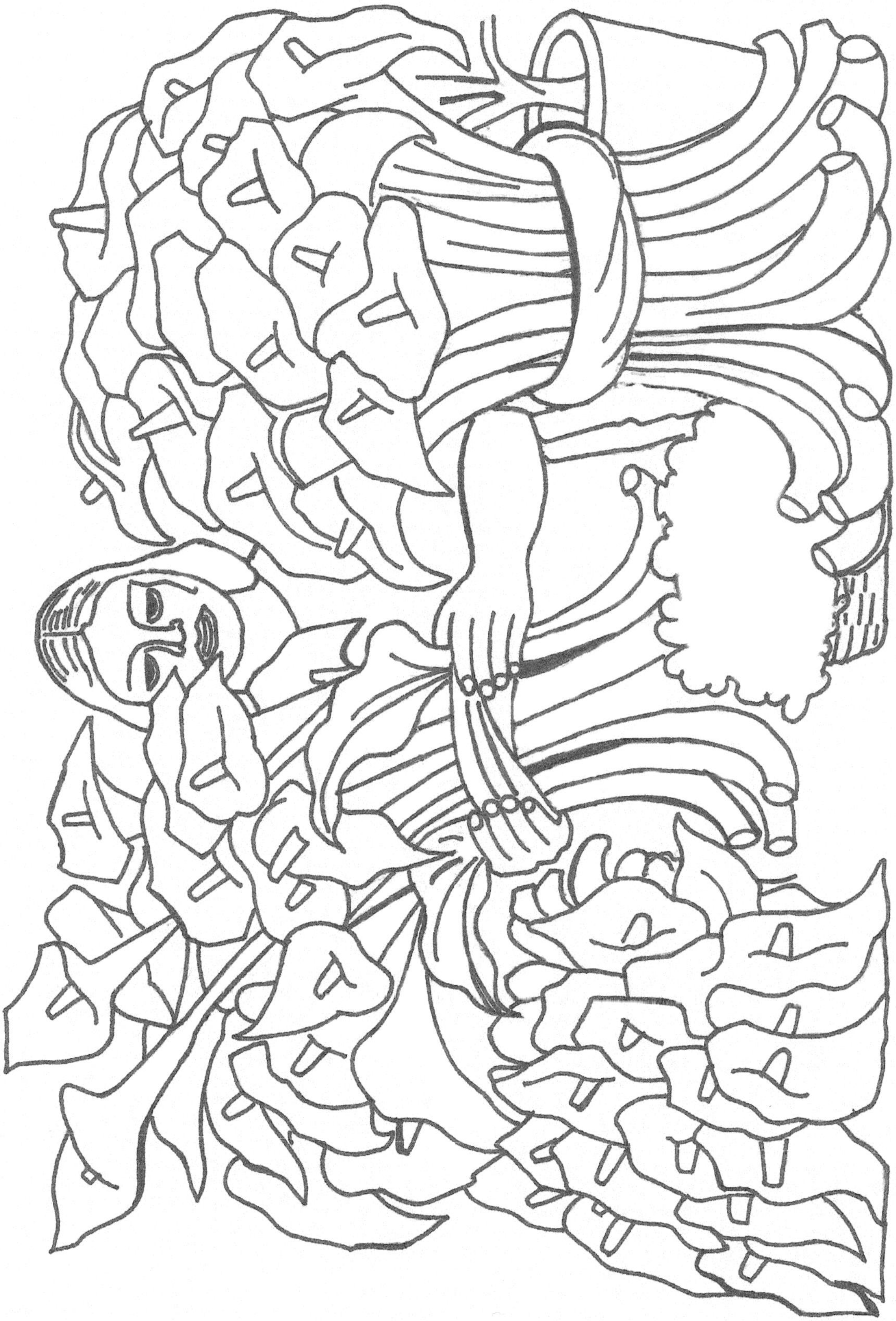

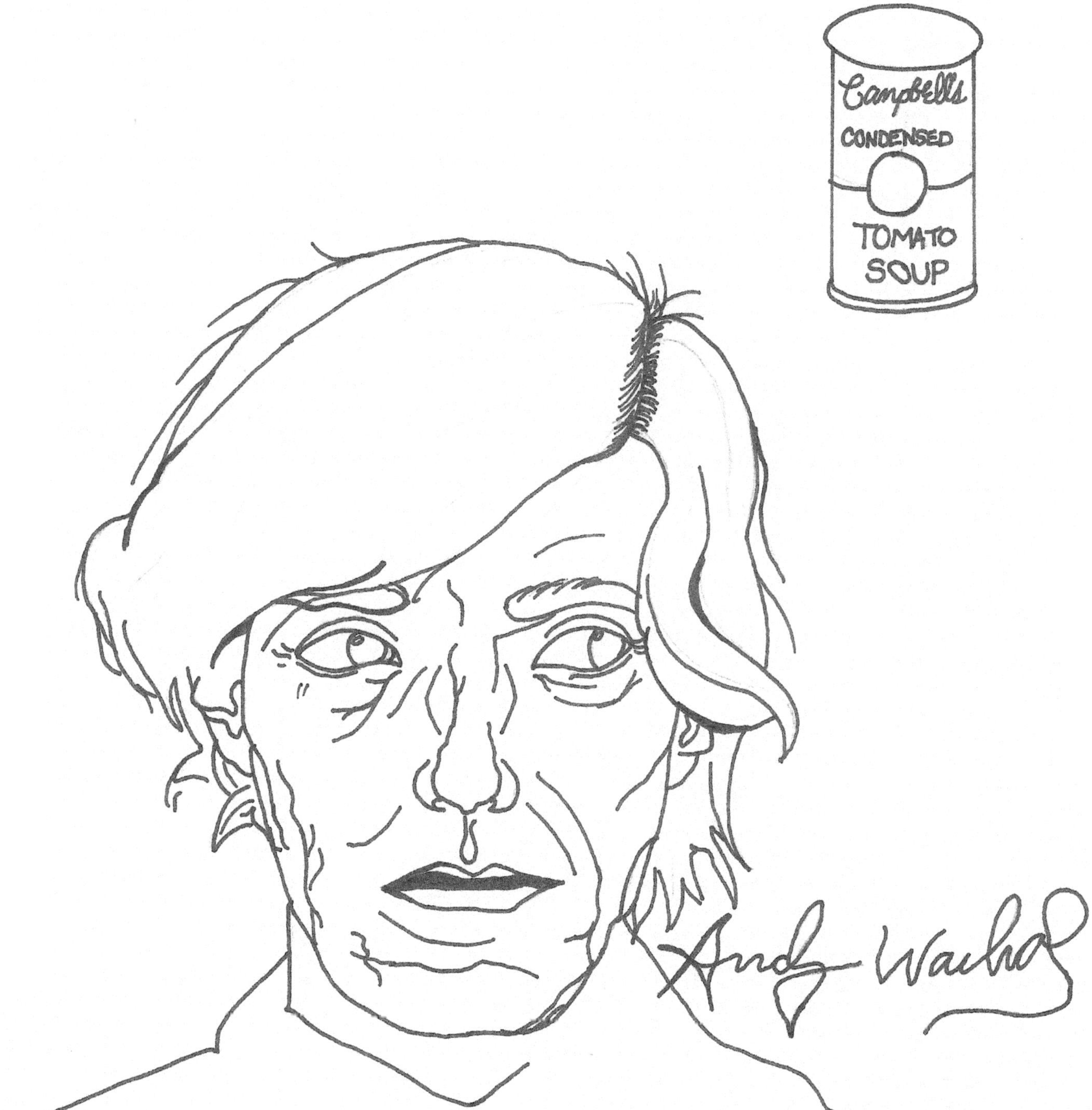
Campbell's
CONDENSED
TOMATO
SOUP
Andy Warhol

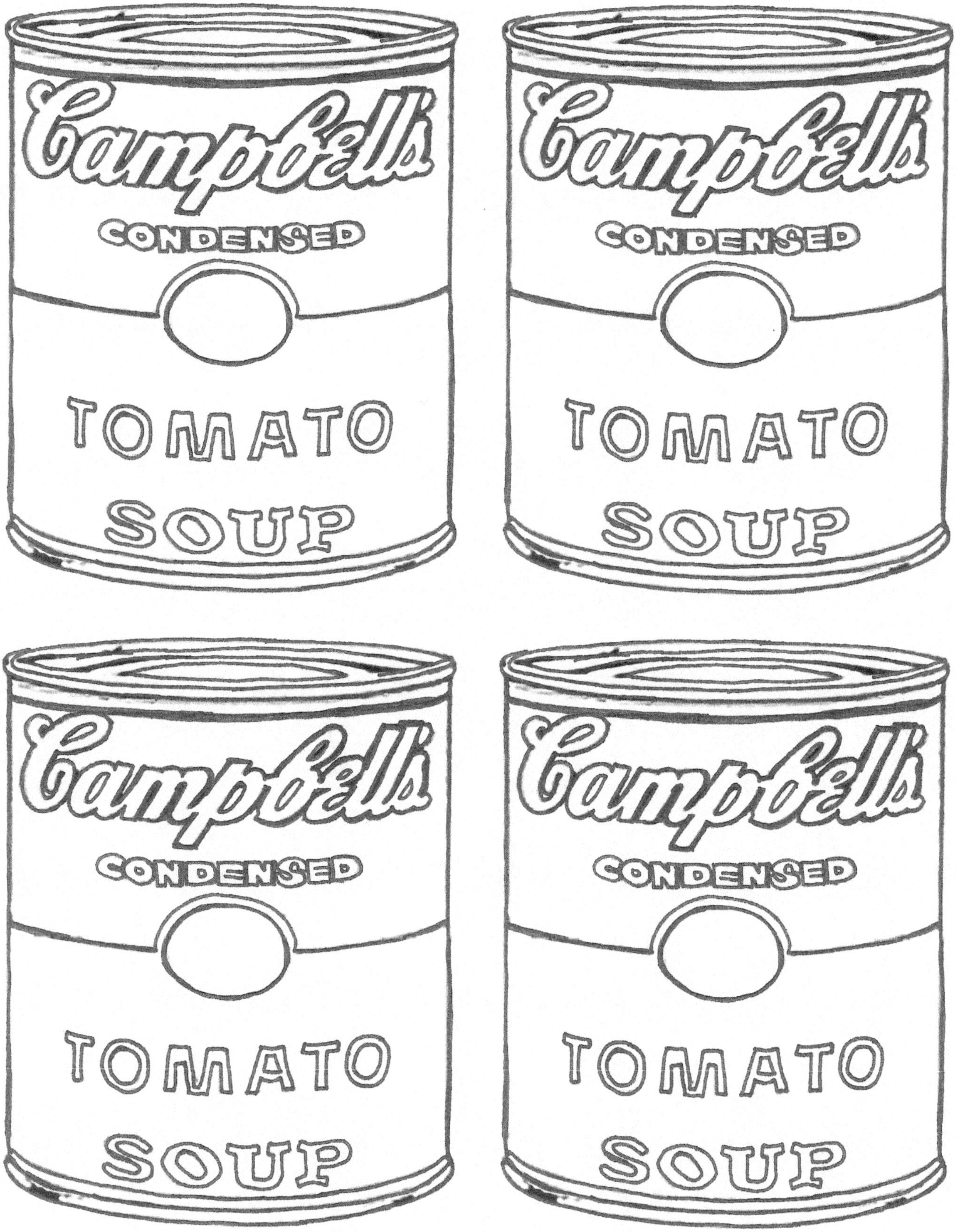
Campbell's
CONDENSED
TOMATO
SOUP
Campbell's
CONDENSED
TOMATO
SOUP
Campbell's
CONDENSED
TOMATO
SOUP
Campbell's
CONDENSED
TOMATO
SOUP

www.ingramcontent.com/pod-product-compliance
Lightning Source LLC
Chambersburg PA
CBHW080602190526
45169CB00007B/2855
* 9 7 8 1 5 3 7 5 5 8 8 5 1 *